MISSIONS
OF CALIFORNIA

CONTENTS

The Spanish missions in California comprise a series of religious outposts established by Spanish Franciscans between 1769 and 1823. The missions represented the first major effort by Europeans to colonize the Pacific Coast region, and gave Spain a valuable toehold in this new frontier. From San Diego to Sonoma, the 21 missions create a unique trail of history of early California. The origin of this historical beginning took shape back in the Old World when the Kings of Spain planned to create settlements in what is now southern California, hundreds of years before the first mission was established in 1769. Shortly after Columbus' landing in the West Indies in 1492, the King of Spain set his sights on expanding the Spanish Empire in the New World. This empire was designed from both a political and religious premise; politically they wanted to control land as other countries were beginning to come to the area and religiously, to instruct the native inhabitants in the Catholic faith. To understand the influence of the missionary system in California, one must realize that within the Spanish Empire, religion and culture were inseparable.

King Charles V of Spain issued laws pertaining to this expansion.
1. Indians would be permitted to live in communities of their own.
2. Indians should be able to choose their own leaders.
3. No Indian was to be held slave.
4. No Indian was to live outside his own village.
5. No Spaniard was to stay in the Indian village for more than 3 days.
6. Indians were to be instructed in the Catholic faith.

It wasn't long before communities began to spring up in Central America and Mexico. Spain began a conquest of the islands of the Pacific, such as the Philippines. Ships of Spain bringing treasures from the Orient needed safe harbors on their return to Spain. In this effort, Monterey Bay in "*Alta*" (Upper California),

was discovered by the explorer Viscaino in 1602. It would be some 150 years later before the string of missions extended from the Mexico coast to present-day Sonoma.

The missions on the coast of Mexico had been established by the Jesuits, a religious order of Catholic Missionaries who had a different set of rules than what was set forth by Charles V, years earlier. Eventually, the missions were run by the Franciscans, a religious order of priests, and their goal was to push north into *Alta* Caliifornia, and establish a mission system along the coast.

Father Junipero Serra was a Francisan priest who led the way. Miguel Serra was born in 1713 to farmers in Majorca, Spain. He was educated at a Franciscan Friary and when he took religious vows in 1730, he took the name Junipero, after a beloved disciple of St. Francis of Assisi, founder of the Franciscan Order of Padres. He volunteered to serve the missions in Mexico, and not long after, he sailed to the New World arriving in Mexico City after walking from the eastern coast of Mexico to the capital city. The Governor of Mexico, Gaspar de Portola, and Serra planned how they were going to extend the Spanish Empire into Upper California. It was a two-fold effort — to establish permanent Spanish settlements, halting Russian exploration and claims to North America's Pacific Coast and the other to Christianize the Indian population.

The first expedition was to get to present-day San Diego. There were 5 segments to this expedition, three ships and two land excursions. All left at different times. When the land travelers reached the site, only 2 ships had shown up. The third was never heard from. The crews and soldiers on board the ships were very ill, suffering from scurvy. In spite of this, in July 1769, the first mission in California was begun. On Presidio Hill, just outside San Diego, stands a cross and on it is written, "Here Father Serra first raised the cross. Here began the first mission, here the first town, San Diego, July 16, 1769."

The chain of missions eventually extended some 650 miles up the coast, the last mission being established in 1823. The plan for the mission sites was to place them a traveling distance of one day apart. At the mission, one would find shelter and a safe place to rest before leaving for the next part of their journey. To mark the trail, tradition has it that the missionaries scattered mustard seeds so their bright yellow flowers would be a marker to guide the early missionaries along the *El Camino Real*, (King's Highway) the name for the trail connecting the missions..

Father Serra spent the rest of his life as head of the Franciscans in Alta California. Although he was over 50 years old, thin, asthmatic and suffering from an old leg injury, he founded 9 missions, including his headquarters, the Mission San Carlos Borromeo at Carmel. He died in 1784 and is buried at the Carmel Mission. After Serra's death, the work of establishing missions passed to Father Fermin Francisco de Lasuén. He founded 9 more and the remaining 3 missions were founded by other padres.

With the onset of the Mexican War for Independence in 1810, Spain decided to limit its growth in the New World due to the costs of sustaining the mission outposts. The last mission was founded in Sonoma in 1823, (northernmost site) and the proposed 22nd mission, Santa Rosa, was canceled in 1827. In the meantime, Russian colonization of the Americas reached its southernmost point with the 1812 establishment of Fort Ross, a fur-trading and agricultural base to supply the Alaskan settlements. It is now present-day Sonoma County, California. It was an active settlement until the 1840s when it was abandoned and sold to John Sutter of Sutter's Fort in the Sacramento Valley.

The Mission Period (1769-1833)

In a span of 54 years, 21 California missions were established near the coast extending 650 miles along the *El Camino Real*, (King's Highway). The founding of a mission involved certain rules and procedures, and months of correspondence through many levels of bureaucracy. This could take years. Once permission was granted to start a mission in a certain area, much thought was given to whether there was a water supply, wood for fires and building as well as grassy fields for grazing animals, fertile soil for growing crops, access to a port and presence of Native American populations. After blessing the site, temporary shelters made of tree limbs and thatch were built. Later these structures became the stone and adobe buildings we see today. Selecting a church site was a priority, usually built on an east-west axis taking advantage of the natural light. Next, they stepped off the measurements for the quadrangle of buildings around a courtyard. These buildings were the living quarters, workshops, storerooms and kitchen.

Indians were brought into the congregation near the mission proper, enticed by various means. No longer free and undisciplined, they ultimately converted into civilized members of colonial society. Once an Indian was baptized, he or she became a *neophyte* (new believer). Lured by curiosity but once confined to mission life, they were no longer free to move about but instead were ruled by the padres who set labor and worship hours.

Although the missionaries might have been caring and well meaning, they did not understand or respect the radically different Native American customs. By European standards the Indians were wild, had no God, no laws, armies or churches. Negative attitudes and treatment of the Indians as inferior people led to mistreatment and abuse.

Mission life was not kind or good for the Indians. Many were killed for unknown reasons and many died from disease and starvation. During the measles epidemic of 1806, 1/4 of the Indian population of the San Francisco Bay area died from the disease and its complications.

Mission Life

Each mission was under the direction of two resident padres. Assisting them was a small contingent of soldiers. Bells were a very important part of daily life at the mission. They were rung at mealtimes, the call to work, the summons to worship, the announcement of baptisms and funerals, the approach of visitors or a ship. A typical day's routine would be prayer and Mass at sunrise, lessons in the Catholic faith, then breakfast. The men and older boys had assigned tasks for the day: building, planting, herding animals, etc. The women had their tasks of cooking, weaving, making soap, laundry, etc. Some of the older and stronger children carried the adobe bricks (weighing 50 pounds or more) to the construction sites. There was much work to be done to make a mission self-sustaining. The missionaries taught the Indians how to plant, plow, irrigate, cultivate and harvest crops. They were also taught how to make adobe bricks, build houses, tan hides, shear sheep, make rope, soap, card wool and weave. The workday was long but a 2-hour siesta was a part of each workday. There were many days free from manual labor, Sundays and holidays, both religious and civil. Missions were like slave plantations, the Indians were forced to work but were not paid wages.

Since the goal of all the missions was to be self-sufficient, farming became the easiest way to provide for the success of the mission community. The most common crops were wheat, barley and corn. Much of this was ground into flour. Although the only indigenous fruit were wild berries, the missionaries brought orange, grape, apple, pear and fig plants to the area. These fruits thrived in the warm California sun. Grapes were used for sacramental wine and trading. The first grape planted was at Mission San Juan Capistrano in 1779. The winery there produced the first wine in Upper California in 1783. Olives were first cultivated at Mission San Diego. Much oil was pressed for mission use and for trading.

The missions had the responsibility of providing the Spanish forts or '*presidios*' with food, clothing and other manufactured goods. At times, this put a strain on the missions, especially in years of drought. The Spanish government kept detailed records of the activities at the mission outposts, both religious and commercial. Reports had to be submitted to the government periodically, reporting baptisms, populations, crop output, herd counts, etc. Livestock became important to sustaining a mission, not only for food but also for wool, leather, and tallow and to provide animals to plow the land. In 1832, at the height of mission life, over 150,000 cattle, 140,000 sheep, goats and swine, 14,000 horses and 1,500 mules were owned by the 21 missions. The original starts of these herds were brought from Mexico. They reproduced rapidly on the lush grasslands surrounding the missions. At times, when the livestock herds grew out of control, extermination was ordered to get rid of the excess so the herds could be managed properly.

The mission was a buzz of activity. Tallow was being rendered in large vats and used to make candles, soap and ointments. Leather was tanned and looms for weaving were in constant use. Bakeries and kitchens prepared thousands of meals every day. All the materials used in building had to be manufactured on the premises. Artisans carved doors and the furniture and tools. Kilns hardened the bricks, pots and dishes.

Access to water was a major factor in a sustained mission. Often aqueducts, spanning miles, brought fresh water from nearby springs and rivers. Large cisterns stored water and gravity fed fountains. The force of flowing water turned the grinding wheels and other machinery. Water to be used for drinking and cooking was filtered through layers of sand and charcoal, making it potable.

Rancho Period (1834-1849)

The period of Spanish prosperity in the New World of Alta California was short-lived, 64 years from the founding of the first mission and only 10 years after the 21st mission was started. When Mexico gained independence from Spain, they could no longer afford to continue supporting the expansion in California, and so, in 1833 after the Act of Secularization was signed, the missions were turned over to civil authorities. The resident padre retained the church, gardens and chapel — all other buildings went to the *pueblo* (town). The Secularization Act ordered the immediate secularization of all the missions in California. The intent of the act was to immediately transfer to the Indian neophytes all of the wealth and property which had been accumulated under the mission system. It was Governor José Figueroa's duty to put the act into operation, but he realized that the mission Indians were not capable of assuming private ownership without a period of supervision and education. Accordingly, he proposed to secularize only ten missions the first year. Half of the lands and livestock would be apportioned to the leading Indian families, who would not be permitted to sell, trade or give them away. The other half would remain under the temporary control of the mission fathers, who were to continue in their religious work. Providing the Indians made good use of their first property over a period of years, the balance of the mission holdings would then be distributed. Eventually, according to Figueroa's plan, the mission chapel would become the parish church in the center of an Indian community. Had Figueroa lived, the plan might have succeeded. However, with his death in 1835, control fell into the hands of greedy politicians who ignored the interest of the Indians, and proceeded to divide the spoils among their friends and relatives.

The Franciscan Friars abandoned most of the missions, taking with them everything of value; the locals then plundered the grounds for construction materials, etc. Fortunately, most of the historical records went to an archive at Mission Santa Barbara, which is still under the control of the Franciscans. It is a center for the study of mission history; Santa Barbara is the only mission that has maintained an uninterrupted presence of Franciscan leaders.

A typical rancho would include a main family house, with attached quarters for the *vaqueros* (well-trained cowboys) and other ranch workers plus structures such as ovens and slaughtering facilities. The rancheros manufactured almost nothing themselves, but slaughtered huge numbers of cattle for hides and tallow in preparation for the trading ships to come into port. Hides were treated as currency. The ships brought tools, furniture, clothing and food staples for trade.

In 1863, President Lincoln returned all the mission lands to the Catholic Church, but by then, most were in ruins. Even though the missions were returned to the Catholic Church, the burden of maintenance left most of the sites in dire condition. Currently, the Catholic Church controls all but 2 missions. Mission La Purisima and Solano are owned and operated by the California Department of Parks and Recreation as State Historical Parks. Seven mission sites are National Historic Landmarks, 14 are listed as National Historical Places and all are California Historic Landmarks because of their historic and architectural significance. The Holy See in Rome has designated four missions, San Diego, Carmel, Dolores and San Juan Capistrano as minor basilicas due to their religious, cultural and architectural importance.

In the late 1880's, artists and authors visiting the missions brought the condition and plight of the missions to the attention of interested people nationwide. William Randolph Hearst and other members of the Landmarks Club of Southern California began to restore 3 of the missions in the early 1900s, namely San Juan Capistrano, San Diego and San Fernando missions. Today the missions exist in varying degrees of architectural integrity and structural soundness. The church itself was always the first focus in restoration. Some compounds remain relatively intact and true to the original structure. The missions' contribution to California history has been recognized as worthy of preservation as much as is possible to the way it was during the Mission Building Era. The restoration is currently directed by The California Missions Foundation, a volunteer, tax-exempt organization. In 2004, President George W. Bush signed HR146, the "California Mission Preservation Act," into law. This measure funds $10 million over a 5-year period to the California Missions Foundation for projects that relate to the preservation of the missions and their artifacts.

Tourists from all over the world visit these gems of history each year. Fourth grade California students study California history and most of them visit a mission during that year. All the missions are open to the public and some have museums. Each mission is unique but with commonalities of purpose and intent. Restoration continues today, keeping this important cultural treasure available for all to visit and enjoy.

Mission San Diego de Alcalâ
San Diego

San Diego de Alcalâ, the first of the 21 great California Missions, marks the birthplace of Christianity in the "New World." Before the early 1500s it was thought that California was an island. In 1542, Juan Rodriguez Cabrillo, a Spanish explorer, arrived in San Diego Bay, naming it San Miguel after the feast day of St. Miguel. In 1602, Sebastian Viscaino, another Spanish explorer, arrived in the bay and renamed it San Diego, after Saint Didacus of Alcalâ Spain. Prompted by stories of Russian seal hunting along the California coast, King Carlos III of Spain became concerned that the Russians would be claiming this area so he decided to proceed to build settlements in "Alta" or Upper California. It was a political move but the King wanted to make it religious so he assigned this undertaking to the Franciscan Friars who were already in charge of several missions in Baja or Lower California. Father Junipero Serra was chosen to lead these expeditions along with a contingent of military under the direction of Gaspar de Portola. Five different expeditions set out at different times from Mexico (New Spain) for the San Diego Bay — 3 ships and 2 land expeditions. Father Serra was in the last land expedition. It was a difficult and hazardous venture. Only 2 ships arrived and most of the passengers were very ill with scurvy after being at sea for 3 months. The supply ship, San Jose, was lost at sea, never heard from again. The land expeditions were difficult and heavy with casualties because they were leading mules and horses, carrying food supplies, plus seeds and farming tools. Of the 219 who started out on the first 5 expeditions, nearly half perished.

Father Serra's group arrived on June 29, 1769. On a site overlooking the bay (known today as Presidio Hill), Father Serra established Mission San Diego on July 16, 1769. The mission remained at this site for only 5 years because the water supply was insufficient for growing crops, the soil was poor and the American Aldians were

being intimidated by the military. The site was moved 6 miles east, close to the San Diego River and the Indian villages (*rancherias*). In 1775, just one year after the first church was built, a few Indians who rebelled against the rules of order of mission life, led a band of 600-800 Indians to storm the mission, plundering and burning the entire mission. The mission pastor, Father Luis Jayme was killed in the process, thus becoming the first Christian martyr in California. He is buried under the altar at the current day Mission Church. Many of the mission residents fled to the garrison on Presidio Hill (the original site).

Father Serra, who had left years earlier, returned to help rebuild. Fearing another attack, this time they built the church and buildings in a quadrangle shape like an army fort. Walls of adobe several feet thick and roofs of tile made them resistant in the event of a future attack and they also served as a protection against the rain.

In spite of its difficult beginning, the mission became very successful. In 1797, some 28 years later, the padres baptized 565 Indians. The mission owned 50,000 acres of land, 20,000 sheep, 10,000 cattle and 1,250 horses. Wheat, corn, beans, wine grapes, barley and beans were cultivated on the vast acreage. Despite the fact that the original animals for the mission came from Mexico and the soil mostly infertile with insufficient water, the mission was very successful.

After 1834, the mission was turned over to Santiago Arguello. During the period 1846-1862, the mission was occupied by the U.S. Cavalry. They took care of the buildings only enough to make them habitable. After being abandoned for several years and in ruins, restoration began in the 1880s by Father Anthony Ubach. Nothing much was done for several years after Father Ubach died in 1907 until the 1930's when a mirror church was built to match the 1813 church. It is the church in use today. The front of the church is plain, perhaps the simplest of all the missions. The *campanaria* (bell tower wall) is beautiful in its simplicity and strength. It has been an active parish church since 1941 and was proclaimed a minor basilica by Pope Paul VI in 1976.

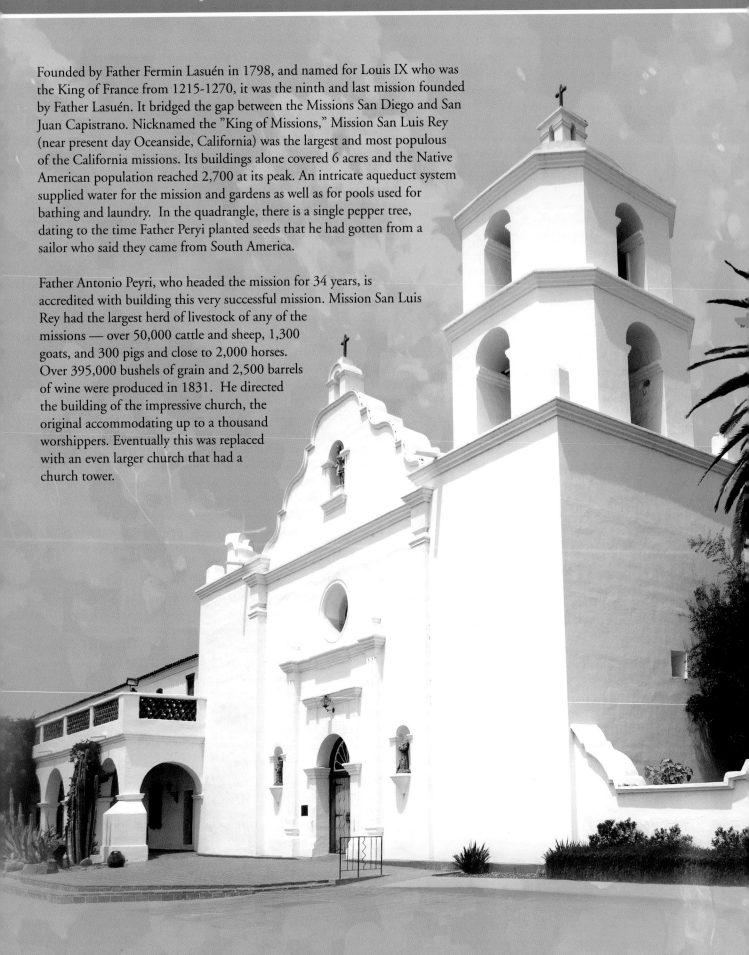

Mission San Luis Rey de Francia
San Luis Rey

Founded by Father Fermin Lasuén in 1798, and named for Louis IX who was the King of France from 1215-1270, it was the ninth and last mission founded by Father Lasuén. It bridged the gap between the Missions San Diego and San Juan Capistrano. Nicknamed the "King of Missions," Mission San Luis Rey (near present day Oceanside, California) was the largest and most populous of the California missions. Its buildings alone covered 6 acres and the Native American population reached 2,700 at its peak. An intricate aqueduct system supplied water for the mission and gardens as well as for pools used for bathing and laundry. In the quadrangle, there is a single pepper tree, dating to the time Father Peryi planted seeds that he had gotten from a sailor who said they came from South America.

Father Antonio Peyri, who headed the mission for 34 years, is accredited with building this very successful mission. Mission San Luis Rey had the largest herd of livestock of any of the missions — over 50,000 cattle and sheep, 1,300 goats, and 300 pigs and close to 2,000 horses. Over 395,000 bushels of grain and 2,500 barrels of wine were produced in 1831. He directed the building of the impressive church, the original accommodating up to a thousand worshippers. Eventually this was replaced with an even larger church that had a church tower.

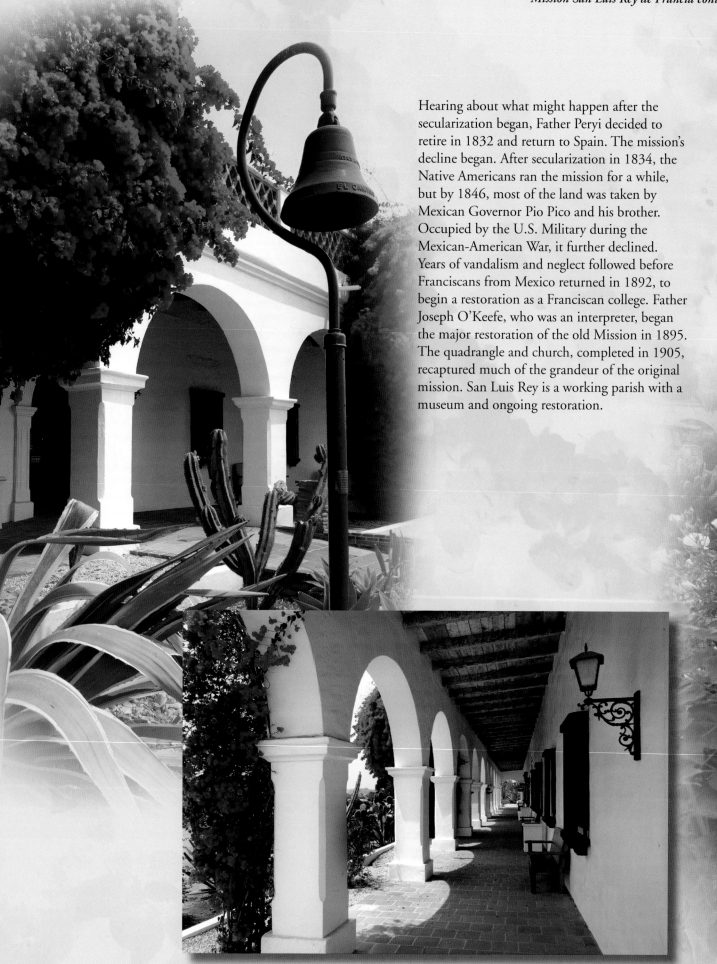

Hearing about what might happen after the secularization began, Father Peryi decided to retire in 1832 and return to Spain. The mission's decline began. After secularization in 1834, the Native Americans ran the mission for a while, but by 1846, most of the land was taken by Mexican Governor Pio Pico and his brother. Occupied by the U.S. Military during the Mexican-American War, it further declined. Years of vandalism and neglect followed before Franciscans from Mexico returned in 1892, to begin a restoration as a Franciscan college. Father Joseph O'Keefe, who was an interpreter, began the major restoration of the old Mission in 1895. The quadrangle and church, completed in 1905, recaptured much of the grandeur of the original mission. San Luis Rey is a working parish with a museum and ongoing restoration.

Established in 1776 by Father Serra, the mission was actually begun a year earlier by Father Lasuén but when he heard about the raid on the San Diego mission and fearing the same outcome for his fledgling mission, he buried the bells and fled to the presidio in San Diego. When Father Serra got there he found the original cross and the buried bells. A little chapel (Serra's Chapel) was built that first year and this is still in use today, the oldest church in California. It is believed to be the only church still standing where Father Serra is known to have said Mass. A great stone church was started in 1796 and finished in 9 years. It was magnificent, 180 feet long and 40 feet wide. A 120-foot bell tower could be seen for miles. It stood for only 6 years until a devastating earthquake in 1812 destroyed it. Tragically, it happened during Mass, killing 40 Native worshipers as well as 2 boys in the bell tower. They

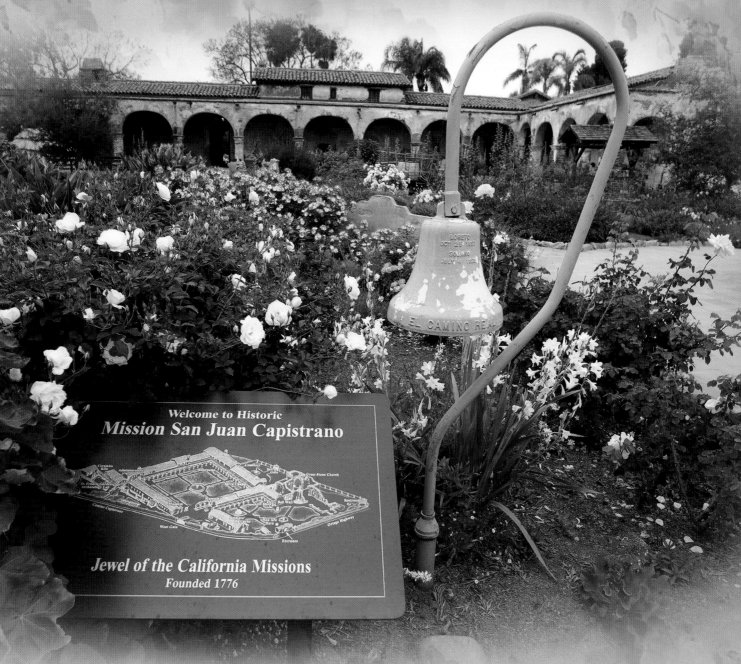

are buried at the mission. Within a year, a brick *campanario* (bell wall) was erected between the chapel and the ruins of the Great Stone church. No plans were made to rebuild.

Called the "Jewel of the Missions," San Juan Capistrano is probably the best known of all the missions. It is famous for its beautiful gardens and for the swallows that migrate each year from some 2000 miles away. Their arrival is celebrated on St. Joseph's Day, March 19, with the ringing of the mission bells.

Historical records reveal this to be a very successful mission. Between 1776 and 1847, 4,639 souls were converted to Christianity and by 1794 over seventy structures were built to provide housing. California's first vineyard was located on the mission grounds and the first wine came from the winery in 1783.

After Mexico's independence from Spain in 1821, there was a gradual decline in the mission growth and maintenance. Disease and natural weather extremes took their toll. After secularization in 1834, Spanish settlers took over the land and most of the Indians gradually left the mission. After 20 years of occupation by the Mexican governor's family members, the mission proper (original buildings, cemeteries,

gardens and acreage) was returned to the Catholic Church by a proclamation signed by President Lincoln in 1863. Attempts were made to restore the mission during the next 30 years, but it wasn't until Fr. John O'Sullivan arrived in 1910 to recuperate from a stroke and seek relief from tuberculosis, that serious attention was paid to preservation. He was fascinated by the extent of the ruins and envisioned restoring this once beautiful mission. His first task was to repair the roof of the chapel. During his time at the mission, the "Sacred Garden" was created in the courtyard adjacent to the stone church. In 1925, the chapel was fully restored. The altar in the chapel is a masterpiece of carved wood and gold inlay and is estimated to be 400 years old. Father O'Sullivan died in 1933 and is buried in the mission cemetery. In the years following, national interest in the missions due to movies, books and art, brought in much needed funds so the restoration could continue.

Mission San Gabriel was founded by Father Pedro Cambón and Father Angel Somera on September 8, 1771. The original plan was to place it on the Santa Ana River, but when the founders arrived, they went further inland to found the mission near the San Gabriel River. The church's design has a strong Moorish influence, probably modeled after the Cathedral of Cordova in Spain. A side campanario holds 6 magnificent bells.

Mission San Gabriel Arcángel was a very prosperous mission but it was also difficult for the padres running it. It was the crossroads for travelers from south to north and east to west. In 1776, the mission was moved again closer to the mountains, present day San Gabriel. This mission produced large crops of wheat, corn and beans. The large herds of cattle provided the items needed for their soap making and tanning hides industries. At times, it furnished food and supplies to settlements and other missions. Well over 25,000 baptisms were conducted between 1771 and 1834, making it the most prolific in the mission chain.

After Mexico won independence from Spain, the missions were secularized. Originally, the lands were supposed to be transferred to the natives, but in the end most of the land fell into the hands of dishonest politicians and their friends, and the place was turned over to a civil administrator in 1834. Within ten years, the San Gabriel Mission was stripped of all its valuables. Governor Pio Pico tried to sell the mission to a friend, but he was stopped when United States troops arrived. In 1863, Congress returned the land to the Catholic Church. Claretan Missionary Fathers came to San Gabriel in 1908 and began restoration. A major portion of the original mission has since been restored. A museum today houses a fine collection of sacred Native American art. The church is open to the public, and the ancient cemetery, the cactus garden, and much of historical interest may be seen on the grounds. Today San Gabriel possesses perhaps the finest collection of mission relics in existence. Its hammered copper baptismal font was the gift of King Carlos III of Spain in 1771. The six priceless altar statues were brought from Spain around Cape Horn in 1791.

The Mission San Fernando provided the stop between San Gabriel and San Buenaventura Missions. It was the fourth mission founded by Father Fermin Lasuén. It was founded on September 8, 1797. The fertile valley became very productive with over 30,000 grape vines and 21,000 head of livestock. In 1804, nearly 1,000 Indians lived at the mission. The Indians at the mission learned the trades of the missions. Blacksmithing, farming, ranching, carpentry, weaving, leather making, brick making, and soap making all became important trades at the mission. Since nails and spikes were very rare, the leather was torn into strips, which were then used in construction. The San Fernando Mission was famous for their grapes and wine.

The City of Los Angeles' population was growing and there was a market for the goods produced at the mission. Since the mission was located along the principal road going to Puebla de Los Angeles, the padres hosted many travelers and so they built a "long building" to accommodate the visitors. It was 243 feet long, 50 feet wide, and 2 stories high with a colonnade of 20 arches. It was the largest adobe building in California.

After secularization in 1834, the mission became headquarters of another of Governor Pio Pico's family and became his headquarters. Further decline came when it became a warehouse, stage station and even a hog farm. The roof tiles were stolen and used in other construction. This left the adobe walls open to the elements and soon they crumbled.
Prospectors, who heard that gold might be hidden there, dug up the floor of the church.

The mission became a working church again in 1923. Many attempts were made to restore the mission but it was not until the Hearst Foundation gave a large gift of money in the 1940s that the church, the "long building", the wine press, smoke room, refectory and the entire quadrangle was finally restored. An earthquake in 1971 caused considerable damage to the church. It was completely rebuilt and finished in 1974.

On March 31, 1782, Father Serra celebrated a High Mass, preached on the Resurrection, and dedicated Mission San Buenaventura (St. Bonaventure). It was the ninth and last founded during his lifetime, and one of six he personally dedicated. The first church burned down and it took the Indians 15 years to build the new church, completing it in 1809. That church still stands today.

The friendly Chumash Indians were happy to live at the mission. They were so friendly that the mission was founded right in their village. The Chumash were expert boat builders, which was helpful as the mission sits on the coast with a view of the ocean. By 1816, the mission had 1,328 Indians living in its compound. Their houses were cone shaped and made of tule grass covering a willow frame. The women were known for their basket making.

A seven-mile-long aqueduct was constructed by the Indians to bring Ventura River water to the mission. With plentiful water the mission

was able to maintain flourishing orchards and gardens. Exotic plants such as bananas, figs and sugar cane were grown. The entire system was destroyed by floods and abandoned in 1862.

The earthquake of 1857 greatly damaged the tile roof and it was replaced with a shingled roof. In 1893, in an effort to "modernize" the church, the residing priest decided to paint over the original art on the walls, cover the ceiling and tile floor and lengthen the windows to let in more light, making the church nothing like it was in the early mission days. In 1957, restoration began and brought the church back to its original style. Today all that is left of the original mission is the church and its garden. Services are still held in the parish church. A small museum at the mission displays Chumash relics and mission period items. Among them are the remains of two old wooden bells, which were used in early ceremonies and are the only ones of this type known in California. Outside the museum building stands an ancient olive crusher.

Today, the mission has been engulfed by the city of Ventura, which grew up after the arrival of the railroad in 1887. The two great Norfolk Island pines that stand before it have an estimated age of well over 100 years.

Santa Barbara was the first mission founded by Father Fermin Lasuén, Father Serra's successor. Father Serra actually dedicated the site (the presidio) in 1782 but could not get permission from the governor to start the mission. Sadly, his dream of having a mission at this site did not happen until after his death. Built on a hill, this site has beautiful views of the ocean. The mission's commanding position and grand proportions, graceful lines and soft blending color all reinforce her title, "Queen of the Missions."

The Chumash Indians, who were hunters and gatherers, inhabited the area. The Chumash were skilled workers and the early missionaries admired their basketry and stone bowls. These skills contributed greatly to the success of the mission. The Indians tended to great herds of livestock that included cattle, sheep, goats, pigs and horses. The first mission buildings were made of logs and thatch. Over time the church was built several times of adobe, each time larger to accommodate the growing population. The largest one, completed in 1794, had 6 side chapels. It was destroyed by an earthquake in 1812. Work then began on the final structure that was 161 feet long, 42 feet high and 27 feet wide. When first built, it had one tower, but in 1833, a second tower was added, making this the only mission with 2 towers. Another earthquake in 1925 damaged the beautiful structure but it was quickly restored. An extensive water system was built by the Indians. A dam, aqueducts, reservoirs and filtering mechanisms provided the means to sustain the mission's population and its agriculture. The fountain and *lavadero* (laundry facilities) are intact and can be seen today. Among the ruins remaining today are the tanning vats, filter house and mill. The largest reservoir, built in 1806, is now a part of Santa Barbara City's water system.

After secularization in 1834, the head of the missions at that time, Father Presidente Narciso Durán, transferred his headquarters to Santa Barbara, bringing with him the repository of some 3000 original documents that pertained to all the missions. This archive is the oldest in California and serves as the most important resource for the study of the missions. Lovely Mission Santa Barbara is the only mission in the California chain remaining under control of the Franciscans without interruption from the day of its founding until the present time. All others were abandoned one by one after the Mexican secularization decrees robbed the missions of their lands and control over the Indians. From 1868 until 1877, the buildings were used for a high school and junior college for boys. A seminary for boys studying to be priests was added and operated until 1968. Today the mission is the Parish of Santa Barbara.

Mission Santa Inés was founded on September 17, 1804, by Father Estevan Tapis, and was named in honor of Saint Agnes, an early Christian martyr of the fourth century. The Spanish for Agnes is *Inés*, hence the name of the church. While still in its formative years, the earthquake of 1812 devastated the mission. They quickly began to rebuild and repair, and in a short time, the mission became prosperous. An elaborate water system was built, bringing water from the nearby mountains to Santa Ynez Valley. The Spanish explorers and missionaries admired the Chumash Indians for their creative abilities, friendliness and hospitality. Because they were skilled craftsmen and industrious workers, the mission thrived, raising abundant crops, growing large herds of livestock and building structures for the work of the mission.

In 1821, when Mexico won its independence from Spain, there began a difficult period for the missions because the new Mexican government basically dropped any support the former Spanish regime had given to the missions. Since the missions supported the local presidios, the soldiers began making demands on the Indians to work long hours without pay, against the wishes of the missionaries. Resentments and frustration arose and an unfortunate incident

in 1824 sparked a revolt when a soldier beat a young Chumash Indian. The Indians from local Santa Barbara and La Purisima Missions joined the Santa Inéz Indians against the soldiers at Santa Inés, resulting in fires and death. The Indians, fearing reprisal, fled the mission to hide. The mission declined rapidly when the Indian work force was no longer available to sustain it.

Secularization of the Missions in 1834 caused the mission system to rapidly come to an end. In 1843, the governor of Mexico, Manuel Micheltorena, tried to stop the secularization – he transferred 35,000 acres of Santa Inés Mission lands to Francisco Garcia y Moreno, the first bishop of Alta California, so a seminary could be established. It continued to educate priests until 1881. Governor Pio Pico, who was not as sympathetic to the missions, illegally sold Mission Santa Inés to José Covarrubias and José Carrillo for $7000. Later, when the United States gained control of California, most of the property was returned to the Church. The mission buildings continued to deteriorate until 1904 when Father Alexander Buckler became pastor and he and his niece, Mamie Goulet, spent the next 20 years faithfully restoring the mission. It was not until 1947 when the Hearst Foundation donated money for the restoration project that most of the restoration was completed. It is an ongoing endeavor and today the mission is an active parish with a museum and gift shop.

Mission La Purisima Concepción
La Purisima

Mission La Purisima, founded on December 8, 1787, is located some distance away from the El Camino Real. It was named in honor of the Immaculate Conception whose feast day is December 8. Father Fermin Lasuén established this 11th mission near the city of Lompoc but after the 1812 earthquake and floods that followed destroyed the entire mission, it was moved to a site 4 miles to the east.

The Chumash were taught the many skills needed to make the mission successful; construction of adobe buildings and water systems, herding livestock, growing crops, weaving and tanning. etc. Other established missions provided the stock and seeds etc., and soon the mission flourished. The mission had 2 padres with 5-6 assigned soldiers as was customary for all missions. In 1804, it is recorded that there were 1520 *neophytes* (newly baptized Christians) at the mission. That same year a new padre, Father Mariano Payeras, who had great dedication and foresight, helped the mission grow in wealth and membership. Some items needed by the missions that they could not make themselves such as bells, china, sugar, tools, etc., were brought from Mexico by ships twice a year. Products made by the missions were used in trade.

At the time of the mission's greatest success, a series of tragedies struck. European diseases such as smallpox and measles began to take its toll. Nearly 500 died. Because of the damage caused by the floods they decided to move the mission 4 miles east. At the new site, the mission complex quickly took shape. It is the only mission not built in a quadrangle shape, but the buildings were built to withstand another earthquake. — the walls were four and a half feet thick reinforced with stones. A large irrigation system with aqueducts, pipes and dams was constructed to get precious water to the complex and land from miles away.

In 1824, the Indians heard about the beating of one of the Indians at the Santa Inés Mission. A revolt ensued and the Indians took control of La Purisima and held it for almost a month. In the end, the Indians lost. Ten years later, after secularization, the mission fell into ruin.

In 1903, Union Oil Company acquired the site and realized the historical importance of the mission. Restoration became a viable project for the National Park Service and over the years donations and purchases of 500 plus acres were accumulated. After much research, the ruins of the original 13 buildings and the water system were restored just as they were during the mission glory days. On December 7, 1941, the mission was dedicated as a State Historical Monument. La Purisima Mission is considered to be the most completely reconstructed of the 21 California Missions.

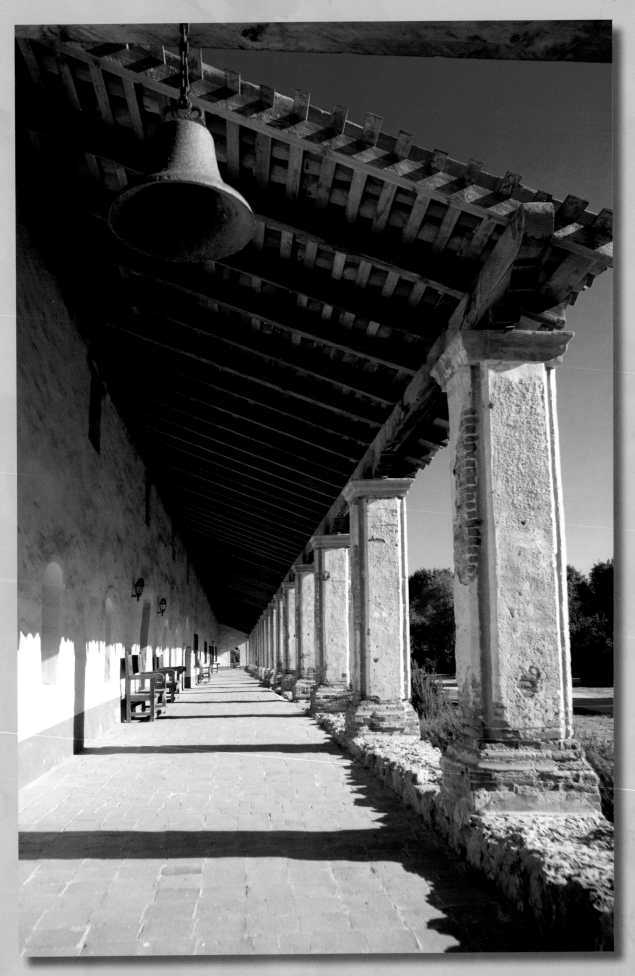

Mission San Luis Obispo de Tolosa was the fifth mission founded by Father Junipero Serra. Started on September 1, 1772, the mission is named for Saint Luis, Bishop of Toulouse, France. The area was known as the "bear plain' because of the abundance of bears in the area. Father Serra left the building of the mission to Father José Cavaller. The Chumash Indians, who were friendly to the missionaries, helped set up temporary buildings made from trees and boughs, but fires were a constant hazard because unfriendly Indians would attack the mission with burning arrows. As the mission grew, more permanent buildings of adobe and tile were built. The red clay roof tiles so familiar to Californians today were first made in California at the mission. The missionaries used this Spanish method to roof their buildings as it was fire proof and it kept the adobe walls and interiors dry. From this date on, all the missions used the red clay tiles for roofs on the mission buildings. The design of the church at the mission is unique in that it is an 'L' shape, unlike the long and narrow naves of other mission churches.

As with most missions, after secularization and lack of support from the Mexican government, Mission San Luis Obispo began to decline. In 1845, Governor Pio Pico sold everything except the church for a total of $510. This meant that the new owner could use the buildings for different uses, namely a school, a jail and the first county courthouse. After California became a state in 1850, Bishop Alemany succeeded in getting the U.S. Government to return the missions to the church. Mission San Luis Obispo was returned to the church in 1859. An attempt to save the mission was made when white siding was put on the church and other buildings. A New England-style steeple was also added.

In 1934, the siding and steeple were removed. This had actually preserved the adobe walls and kept them from further deterioration. Under the direction of Father John Harnett, the buildings underwent extensive restoration to transform them back to early-mission style. Today, the mission is in the heart of downtown San Luis Obispo and serves as a parish church.

On July 25, 1797, Mission San Miguel was founded in a valley near the juncture of the Salinas and Nacimiento Rivers. This site was half way between San Luis Obispo and San Antonio Missions, which were a 2-day journey apart. A church built in 1806 was lost to fire and it took until 1816 to complete the adobe and tile permanent structure that was 144 feet long, 27 feet wide and 40 feet high. The church walls were covered with frescos painted by a few Indians who were taught this art form by Estevan Munras of Monterey. These can be seen today, unretouched, almost 200 years later.

After secularization in 1834, the mission changed when the mission was turned over to civil authorities and all but the church was sold. The

EST. 1797
MISSION
SAN MIGUEL
ARCANGEL
NATIONAL HISTORIC LANDMARK - 2006

Indians left to return to their homelands scattered along the Central Coast. The abandoned mission was sold to the Reed family who lived there until all 11 members were murdered by thieves looking for gold. The buildings were then converted into commercial enterprises — a saloon, hotel and retail stores.

In 1859, the mission was returned to the Church. A priest was assigned to the mission and it served as a mission parish. In 1928, the mission was returned to the Franciscans and is still in their care. An earthquake in 2003 caused extensive damage to the church and it had to be closed for restoration. The church has one of best-preserved interiors of all the missions. Restoration is ongoing.

Father Junipero Serra founded San Antonio de Padua Mission, the third in the chain of 21 missions, in an oak-studded valley east of the Santa Lucia Mountains. On July 14, 1771, the site was dedicated. A bronze bell was hung from a tree branch and rung vigorously by Father Serra himself, calling 'All the Gentiles' to come and worship. Just a few days later, the local Salinan Indians came and accepted beads and cloth from the padres and offered seeds and acorns in return. The mission grew steadily and was moved a little farther north in order to have access to a water supply. An extensive irrigation system was built to bring water from the San Antonio River three miles away to reservoirs and crops. Water was used to run the gristmill, grinding grain into flour. It was the first gristmill in California. Under the direction of Padres Miguel Pieras and Buenaventura Sitjar, the mission flourished. In 1774, only 3 years after its founding, there were 178 Indians, 68 cattle and 7 horses. By 1805, there were 1300 Indians living at the mission, 7,362 cattle, 11,000 sheep, and 800 horses. The harvests of wheat, corn and beans were large and the wine and basket making were thriving industries. The Indian population began to decline after 1805 due to disease. The final church building was started in 1810 and was completed in 1813.

When the last resident priest at San Antonio Mission died in 1882, the buildings were abandoned and deterioration left much of the mission in ruins. The tiles from the roofs had been sold to the Southern Pacific Railroad and used on a mission-style train station in present day Burlingame. The first attempt at

First Marriage in California took place at this Mission between Juan Maria Ruiz of El Fuerte, Sonora Mexico, 25 years of age, and Margarita de Cortona, 22, a Salinan woman of Mission San Antonio, on the sixteenth of May in the year of Our Lord 1773.

restoration came in 1903, when the California Landmark League rebuilt the church walls. However, another earthquake in 1906 damaged what had been rebuilt. In 1928, the Franciscans returned to the mission. The restoration began in earnest again in 1948 when the mission received a grant of $50,000 from the Hearst Foundation.

Today the mission is largely a reconstruction rather than a preserved ruin. The timbers used in the reconstruction were cut and shaped with tools like the ones used in original construction. Much of the elaborate water system is still visible. Because of its remote setting and absence of a town close by, Mission San Antonio is considered to be one of the largest and most picturesque of all the missions. Without the cars of visitors in the parking lot, one can easily imagine mission life as it was in 1790, over 200 years ago.

The mission is surrounded by the Fort Hunter Liggett Military Reservation, which was acquired by the Army from Hearst in the 1940s to train troops. It is still actively training troops today. Although a little difficult to reach, a visit to this mission is well worth the effort.

Mission Nuestra Señora de la Soledad
Soledad

Nuestra Senora de la Soledad Mission was founded by Father Fermin Lasuén on October 9, 1791, the 13th in the chain of 21 missions. The name, *Our Lady of Solitude*, tells a lot about this mission. The dry, windy plain that was very hot in summer and freezing cold on winter nights and with very few Indians, became the mission location between Mission Carmel and Mission San Antonio. An irrigation system brought water from the Salinas River to the dry mission land. Due to the inhospitable weather and land, plus the lack of a large local Indian population to construct the buildings and herd the livestock, growth was slow. Floods from the Salinas River destroyed the church on 3 different occasions. The third one, in 1832, seemed to be the beginning of the end of Mission Soledad. It was difficult to keep the padres happy here. They complained of the poor climate and many ended up in poor health. In spite of all the difficulties the mission faced, they did prosper, converting over 2000 Indians, harvesting bountiful crops and raising large herds of livestock.

Father Vicente Francisco de Sarria, served as the last pastor of Soledad. He served the few remaining Indians at the mission until his death in 1835. After secularization in 1834, what was left of the mission was sold for $800. The mission and 42 surrounding acres were returned to the Catholic Church in 1859. This left the mission abandoned for 100 years. Nothing was left but a few stubs of adobe marking the church walls.

Finally, in 1954, the Native Daughters of the Golden West began restoring what little was left of the Mission Soledad. The location of the church, which was washed away in a flood, was discovered under layers of silt; the tile floor intact. Today a small wing of seven rooms and a small chapel can be visited. The original quadrangle is gone, but the lines can be traced in the mounds of adobe ruins. The area is now a garden. Continued restoration is made possible through donors, proceeds from the gift shop and fundraisers. Today the mission is a part of the Catholic Parish of Soledad but no parish priest is assigned to the mission.

Mission San Carlos Borromeo de Carmelo
Carmel

Father Serra's second mission was established June 2, 1770, after a year of a difficult journey from Mission San Diego to Monterey Bay. Because some of the soldiers at the nearby Presidio were treating the Indians badly, the Indians were reluctant to come to the mission so Father Serra moved the mission to its current site in Carmel, some 5 miles away. This was also a better site for a water source and better land for growing crops. The first church structure was made of wood and mud. The early years at the mission were very difficult because they depended on supplies to come on ships from Mexico and often the expected ships did not arrive. The Indians shared what little supplies and food they had. As time went on the mission began to grow their own food supply and the original buildings were replaced with adobe structures. Carmel became the headquarters for Father Serra and all the missions. It was here that he oversaw the building of seven other missions. Father Serra died here on August 28, 1784, not seeing the prosperity of the missions he founded. He is buried under the altar of the mission.

Father Lasuén continued the work started by Father Serra. Under his leadership, the adobe church was rebuilt using stone from the local Santa Lucia Mountains, making it the first mission built of stone. The ceiling in the church is different from all the others in that the walls taper inward forming a *catenary* arch rather than the usual flat ceiling. Only two other missions used stone in their churches, namely Santa Barbara and San Juan Capistrano. The remaining buildings at the mission today have been rebuilt on the same foundations of the buildings built by Father Lasuén so the layout of the mission today is much like it was in the early 1800's. Father Lasuén died in 1803 and is also buried in the stone church.

After secularization occurred in 1834, the lands were sold. The Indians left to go back to their native lands or to work

on the new owners rancheros. The padres left as mission life was over. The buildings fell prey to vandalism and decay. The adobe-walled quadrangle become piles of mud. The stone church, with its roof caved in, stood in ruin.

Restoration of the mission began in 1884 and continues to this day. The greatest restoration came in 1933 when Mr. Harry Downie was put in charge of the mission restoration. Due to his diligence in restoring it to the original, he was able to gather a great collection of mission artifacts that are now housed in the padre's quarters.
Today the south and west sides of the quadrangle house the Junipero Serra Elementary School.

The careful restoration and beauty of the gardens make Carmel Mission an outstanding historic landmark. The Moorish influence in the architecture is unique. It was designated a Minor Basilica in 1961. In 1987, Pope John Paul II visited the mission as part of his U.S. tour. Today it is an active parish church.

On June 24, 1797, Father Fermin de Lasuén, Presidente of the California Missions following Junipero Serra, began Mission San Juan Bautista. It was named in honor of St. John the Baptist, whose feast day was June 24th. The friendly and cooperative indigenous people provided the manpower to build an adobe church, a granary, barracks, a monastery and some houses. By 1803, a cornerstone was laid for the church as it looks today. It became the widest of all the mission churches (72 x 188 feet) with three aisles and space for 1000 worshipers. It took nearly nine years to complete. Fearing that the walls with large open arches separating the aisles could not withstand an earthquake, the padres decided to abandon the side aisles and fill in the wall arches separating the two outer sides from the main aisle of the church. Later, the tile floor was installed and the main altar and *reredos* (a screen or decoration of religious icons behind an altar) were completed by Thomas Doak, a sailor who had jumped ship in Monterey. He did the painting for room and board.

Talented Father Pedro Estévan Tápis, who had great music ability, joined Father Cuesta at the Mission in 1815 to teach singing to the Indians. He created a system using colors for the different music notes. His choir of Native American boys performed for visitors and the mission became known as "the Mission of Music." Two of his handwritten music books are preserved at the mission museum.

After secularization in 1834, the mission property was seized by the Mexican government, and then in 1859 the present mission and 55 acres were given back to the Catholic Church by a federal decree of the U.S. government.

Earthquakes in 1800 and 1906 were devastating to the mission buildings. The first restoration was attempted in 1884. However, it wasn't until 1949, when the Hearst Foundation donated funds, that restoration began in earnest.

The Old Mission San Juan Bautista has had an unbroken succession of pastors since its founding on June 24, 1797. The altar statues, faux-marble painted wall decoration, huge sandstone baptismal font, and tile floor are all original. Just inside the massive carved entrance doors, on the old red tile floor, you can see 180-year old animal paw prints, probably left by some wandering pets before the tiles dried. There is a cat door in one of the side doors, left over from a time when cats kept mice away. In 1976, a *campanario*, was erected (or possibly rebuilt) in the style of the other missions. Originally nine bells hung outside the church, but only three bells remain. Today, Mission San Juan Bautista is part of a State Historic Park. It faces a plaza much like the one from the late nineteenth century. It includes a hotel, stable and two adobe mansions, all original buildings over 100 years old.

Mission Santa Cruz (Holy Cross) was founded on September 25, 1791, the twelfth in the chain of missions. The site was chosen because of its lush vegetation and forest of redwoods. Prosperous missions that were already established donated supplies and food, etc., to get the mission started. Work began on the church in 1793. It had a stone foundation and five-foot thick walls. It was 112 feet long and 29 feet wide. This would be their church for 65 years. In the beginning years of the mission, the crops flourished, livestock numbers grew and converts to Christianity increased.

After six years of growth and prosperity, things became difficult for the mission. The governor of Alta California decided to build a *pueblo* (town), Villa de Branciforte, just across the river from the mission. The new settlers bribed the Indians with money to get them to work for them, building structures and growing crops. Some stole livestock from mission grounds. Branciforte attracted some unsavory inhabitants and it wasn't long before it became the center of gambling, drinking, smuggling and other crime. The padres were very frustrated, as some of the neophytes were leaving the mission. In an effort to discourage the mission Indians from leaving, those they found in the puebla were severely punished. This, of course, accelerated the mission decline. Many of the Indians who remained at the mission came down with diseases such as measles and scarlet fever. Those who could, ran away in fear of getting the deadly diseases and to escape the punishments and slave-like conditions.

O CRVX AVE
SPES VNICA

CHAPEL OF
MISSION
SANTA CRUZ

Replica of the original
mission at half size.

As with all missions, in 1834, Mexico ordered the missions be turned over to civil authorities. The land was supposed to be given to the Indians but in reality most of the lands were sold or given to local settlers. Usually the mission buildings remained empty and soon began to deteriorate. Earthquakes and erosion contributed to the mission buildings' demise. The earthquake in 1857 completely destroyed the church. In 1858, a wood frame church was built and in 1889, another church, Holy Cross, with high steeples (Gothic Style) was built on the site of the original mission church. Many of the original adobe structures became the beginning of the pueblo of Santa Cruz. In 1931, with a donation from Gladys Sullivan Doyle, a small replica of the original mission church (half-size of original) was built near the original site.

There is nothing left of the original mission structures except for a row of buildings that one time housed the local Yokut and Ohlone Indian families. This 180-year-old building became the headquarters for the Santa Cruz Mission State Historic Park. The museum opened in 1991.

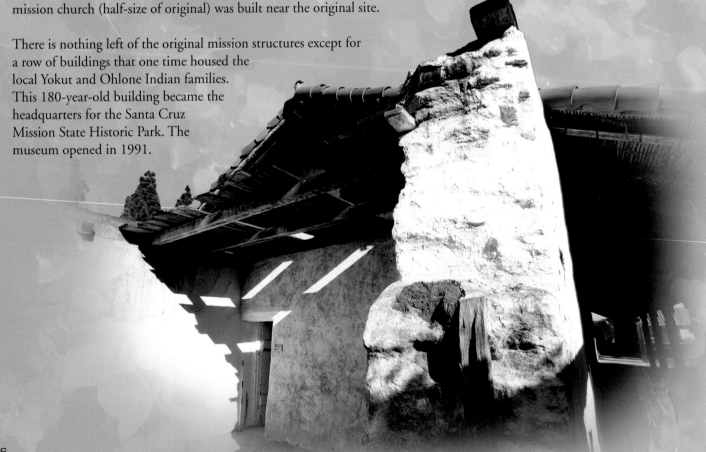

Mission Santa Clara de Asís, the first mission to be christened after a woman, St. Clare of Assisi, was founded on January 12, 1777, by Father Junipero Serra. It occupied five different locations. The first site near the Guadalupe River proved to be a poor choice because of periodic flooding. The second site was temporary until a third site could be found and blessed by Padre Serra himself. Completed in 1784, the third church was an imposing adobe structure 100 feet long, 22 feet wide and 20 feet high with 4-foot-thick adobe walls. Interestingly, in 1911, a man digging for a gas line accidentally found the cornerstone and its contents. The cornerstone and its contents are on display in the Mission Room of the University's de Saisset Museum. This site stood for 34 years until an earthquake in 1818 devastated the buildings. Finally, a fifth and present mission site was begun in 1822. The only remaining structures from this period are now known as the Adobe Lodge and the Adobe Wall. The Adobe Lodge houses the University's Faculty Club.

The missionaries served the Costanoan or Ohlone Indians who were hunters and gatherers, leading a peaceful life and living in harmony with their environment. The missionaries' goal was to make good Spanish citizens out of the Indian populations. They taught the women how to cook and make clothing; the men learned farming, building, herding livestock and tending orchards and olive groves. In spite of the difficulties in its early mission life, the mission became prosperous. By 1800, there were 1,247 Indians living at the mission. By 1827, the mission owned over 14,000 head of cattle, and over 15,000 head of sheep. The mission supplied food and products to the nearby pueblo and presidio as well as the large mission community.

As with all missions, secularization required the missions be turned over to civil authorities and the lands given to the Indians. Unfortunately, the Indians were defrauded of their land and livestock. At Santa Clara, the Franciscan pastors operated it as a parish during the 1830s and 1840s. Rev. Alemany, bishop of California during this time, knew there was a great demand for schools due to the influx of new

settlers arriving during the gold rush so he turned over the decrepit mission buildings to the Jesuits in March 1851. Within months, the first college in the State of California began instructing students. It was named Santa Clara College. A shortage of teachers and money plus the legal difficulties of ownership plagued the early years of the college. The University of Santa Clara, still operated by Jesuits, is the only mission to become part of a university.

Over the years, several remodels of the 1828 mission church changed the façade. A fire in 1926 destroyed the 1828 mission structure; a rebuilt reproduction of Mission Santa Clara (as it was in 1828) was completed in 1929 and now serves as the chapel on the campus. The big wooden cross that was erected in 1777 still stands in front of the Church. The bell tower contains the original bells sent from Spain so long ago. The bells are rung each evening at 8:30 pm as they have for over 225 years.

Mission San Jose
San Jose

Mission San Jose was established on June 11, 1797, the only mission east of San Francisco Bay. It is located along the natural highway through the Livermore Valley to the San Joaquin Valley. The peaceful hunter and gatherer Ohlone Indians inhabited this area. Under the direction of Father Narciso Durán, who arrived in 1806, the mission flourished. The fertile soil, sources of water, stones and soil that was good for making adobe bricks, all helped the success of Mission San Jose. By 1832, the mission's lands extended from present day Oakland to San Jose. Great harvests of wheat, grapes and olives and the thousands of cattle, horses and sheep that roamed the plains made Mission San

Jose one of the wealthiest of all the 21 missions. By 1816, much of the Indian-made goods were traded for sugar, spices, coffee, hardware, tools and supplies. Records indicate 2000 Indians were living at the mission in 1830. Father Durán was musically talented and taught the Indians to read music and play instruments. The band and choir performed for audiences who came from miles away.

After secularization in 1834, the mission was no longer active and in the hands of the missionaries so the Indians fled and the buildings began to decline. Many of the Indians found it difficult to return to their former way of life and many died of disease and starvation. During the gold rush of the mid 1800s and statehood in 1850, the mission was converted to a place of lodging and a commercial general store.

The permanent adobe church was started in 1805. It was a simple building with very thick walls. It was dedicated in 1809. It served the large Indian population until 1868 when an earthquake destroyed it. In 1869, a wooden Gothic-style church was built on the foundation of the original church. It served as a Catholic parish church until 1965. Later, it was carefully relocated to San Mateo to serve the needs of the Episcopal Church. Since it was built on the foundation of the original adobe church, it had to be moved.

The original mission complex consisted of over 100 buildings. In 1950, an effort by the Native Sons and Daughters of the Golden West saved a surviving portion of the mission, converting it to a museum. After much archaeological investigation, plans to reconstruct the church began in 1973. A replica of the 1809 adobe church was begun in 1982. Great attention was given to the authenticity of the church, using

old timbers and rawhide thongs instead of nails and making the walls 4 to 5 feet thick using handmade adobe bricks. The interior decorations follow what was found in the archives and inventories that were recorded in the early days of the mission. The near-perfect replica does hide a steel frame, which provides protection against earthquakes.

Today, further restoration continues with plans to restore the surviving adobe wing and the padres' living quarters. St. Joseph's is an active parish with an elementary school.

In spring of 1776, a scouting party from Monterey visited the area near San Francisco Bay and named the small stream and lake *Arroyo de Nuestra Senora de los Dolore*s (Lake of Our Lady of Sorrows). The first church in San Francisco was built nearby; it was a crude structure, actually an arbor built by the Spanish soldiers in June 1776, which later became the site of Mission Dolores. The founding date is listed as June 29, 1776. When the ship with supplies arrived in August work began in earnest on the mission buildings.

Because the location had limited space available for crops in addition to the harsh weather, progress at the mission was slow. The Indians found the attractions at the nearby presidio and nearby pueblo more interesting than the demands made on them at the mission. Those Indians who had contracted European diseases such as measles found it impossible to get well in the cold and damp climate

of the area. It is thought that 5000 Native Americans were buried on the mission grounds. In 1817, the large numbers dying from the measles epidemic led the missionaries to build a hospital in San Rafael, which was more inland and offered a warmer and drier climate. Later this became the Mission San Rafael Arcángel, the last of the 21-mission chain.

 In 1782, the mission was moved to a more favorable site about a block and a half west. In 1791, the beautiful new adobe church was dedicated. It was built so well that it withstood the 1906 earthquake. Today it is the oldest intact building in San Francisco.

Secularization in 1834 brought the mission life to a close. The livestock and lands were sold off and only the church, padres' quarters and small amount of land were left to stay with the missionaries. The California Gold Rush of the 1850s brought many settlers to the area. The mission became surrounded by saloons, gambling halls, and hotels; some of the mission buildings were converted to a tavern and way station for travelers. In order to serve all the new settlers, a large Gothic Revival brick church was built on the mission grounds in 1876. The old adobe church was covered with wood siding to protect it and to make it look "better." It was removed when the restoration began.

The earthquake of 1906 destroyed the Gothic Revival brick church. In 1913, construction was started on a new church now known as Mission Dolores Basilica. The original mission church was 22 feet wide, and was constructed of adobe bricks set in very thick walls and sitting on a foundation of rock 4 feet below the surface. The façade is unique among the missions. It appears to have four huge columns supporting a second story balcony housing 6 more columns and 3 bells. The roof timbers are still lashed together with rawhide. Today, both the mission church and nearby basilica serve the people in the heart of San Francisco.

On December 14, 1817, Father Vicente de Sarria founded an *asistencia* (sub-mission) to serve as a hospital for the Indians suffering from diseases at Mission Dolores. It was named Mission San Rafael Arcángel, the patron of good health. It was thought the warmer, sunnier climate would help the sick to recover. As word spread that this location did help many recover, other missions began sending their sick to San Rafael. It was given full mission status on October 19, 1822.

The mission grew and became prosperous. The population reached to over 1000 in the short time the mission existed. It is one of only two missions not having a quadrangle. It was one of the first missions to be turned over to the Mexican government when secularization was declared in 1833.

By 1844, the mission was abandoned and what was left of the empty buildings was sold in 1846. John C. Fremont used it as his headquarters during the *Bear Flag Revolt* — the battles fought to make California a United States territory. In 1861, a new parish church was built near the old chapel ruins. In 1870, the remaining ruins were removed to make room for the city of San Rafael. All that was left of the mission was a single pear tree from the old mission orchard. The old church was rebuilt and restored in 1949 by Monsignor Thomas Kennedy. Today that church sits next to the St. Raphael Parish, which was built on the site of the original hospital.

Between the dates of the construction of the adobe mission buildings (which began the spring following the founding in 1817, and continued over a 15-year period) until the razing of those structures in 1861, no one sketched or painted those buildings so no one really knows if the rebuilt adobe church is as it was in 1830.

The last and northernmost California mission, Mission San Francisco Solano was the only mission founded after Mexico gained their independence from Spain. It was established on July 4, 1823, by Father Jose Altimira, who did so without the permission of the Mission Presidente. He was encouraged by the governor who wanted a buffer between the prosperous Bay area settlements and the Russians who had come down the coast as far as Fort Ross.

In contrast to Mission Dolores where the inclement weather became a problem, Mission Solano had a warmer, sunnier climate and it was easier to attract and keep the Native Americans content. Vineyards did well here. Unfortunately, the cruel punishments of Father Altimira, the mission padre, led to a revolt by the Native Americans in 1826. After looting and burning the buildings and supplies, Father Altimira wanted to be transferred to another mission, but no one wanted him so he returned to Spain. A priest from the San Jose mission, Father Buenaventura Fortuni, came to Mission Solano. He was a kind and loving man and soon had the mission under control. He oversaw the construction of most of the buildings on the mission grounds. On one side of the quadrangle was a *convento* (dormitory) with 27 rooms for the priests and guests. At its peak, over 10,000 acres were being used to raise sheep, cattle and crops. In the short time the mission existed, only 11 years, it became prosperous and self-sustaining.

After secularization in 1834, the mission came under the control of General Mariano Vallejo who was supposed to distribute the land and its assets to the Indians, but instead took them for himself, which expanded his holdings to include the pueblo Sonoma. He promised the Indians protection, room and board and put them to work on his ranchos.

The original adobe church collapsed in the late 1830s due to neglect. It was replaced by a smaller adobe chapel in 1841. Much of the remaining buildings had deteriorated with settlers taking the tiles, timbers and adobe bricks to use in their own construction. In 1881, it was sold for $3,000 and another larger church was built nearby.

In 1903, the original adobe mission was sold to the California Landmarks League for eventual preservation. With state funds, they restored the mission chapel and in 1926, they turned the property over to the state. It is now the Sonoma Mission State Historic Park, consisting of 36 acres in the city of Sonoma, California. Extensive archaeology diggings in the 1950s have uncovered much about the early mission that is not yet restored.